MY
LETTER
TO
JERRY

A BRIEF LOOK
AT GOD'S JUSTICE

"JIMAKY" JAMES EDWIN

WESTBOW
PRESS®
A DIVISION OF THOMAS NELSON
& ZONDERVAN

WestBow Press books may be ordered through booksellers or by contacting:

WestBow Press
A Division of Thomas Nelson & Zondervan
1663 Liberty Drive
Bloomington, IN 47403
www.westbowpress.com
844-714-3454

ISBN: 978-1-6642-9955-9 (sc)
ISBN: 978-1-6642-9956-6 (e)

Library of Congress Control Number: 2023908522

Print information available on the last page.

WestBow Press rev. date: 05/11/2023

CONTENTS

"Come, all you who are thirsty, come to the waters;
and you who have no money, come, buy and eat!
Come, buy wine and milk without money and without cost.
Why spend money on what is not bread, and
your labor on what does not satisfy?
Listen, listen to Me, and eat what is good, and
your soul will delight in the richest of fare.
Give ear and come to me; hear Me, that your soul may live.
I will make an everlasting covenant with you,
My faithful love promised to David."
Isaiah 55:1–3, NIV

The above is a copy of an ancient text,
written over 2,500 years ago.
In it there is a profound mystery still in effect today.
It's what this letter is all about.

I want to express my gratitude to all of these
mentioned below, beginning with
The Lord, Jesus Christ, for what He has done for
all of us. He is the central focus of this letter.
And to my family, beginning with my sweet wife, Elizabeth.
Without her, I would be without my best friend. She is my
partner in life and God's blessing to me. You and I have grown
together in Christ, and your faith is an inspiration to me.
My daughter, Jennifer, her husband, Chad, and
their three amazing children: Abigail Grace,
Chandler Wayne, and Brooklyn Kate.
My son, Samuel, his wife, Ashley, and their
three amazing children: Adelyn Grace, Braden
"Chuck" Charles, and Lovelyn Rose.
I must also recognize and acknowledge my extended family,
which includes my brothers and sisters of the First Methodist
Church in Tulsa, especially the "One in the Spirit Class."
And to all my brothers who meet on Wednesday mornings for
bible study, you are the "iron that sharpens iron," and my life
would not be the same without your friendship and fellowship.
I also want to recognize my friend and employer, the architect
with whom I have worked for the past fifty years, Jack Arnold.
After all those years working together, he is more of a brother
than a boss. And it was at his conference table that I met Jerry.

And, of course, I couldn't leave out my friend Jerry,
to whom this letter is written. Thank you, my friend,
for prompting me to write all this down.

PREFACE

I met Jerry at a conference table in my office several years ago. He was the general contractor constructing a small office building our firm had designed. I'm an architect, and I usually sit down with those who are involved in our building projects. There are often questions and answers during the construction phase, and this was no exception. What turned out to be somewhat of an exception is the friendship he and I developed. During one of our meetings, our conversation shifted from the project to life in general and to the struggles we all face at times.

At the close of that meeting, I asked Jerry if we could pray about the things we had discussed. His face lit up, and he said, "Absolutely!" That prayer brought our friendship to a new level. Over time, as the office building progressed, Jerry would bring a sack of sandwiches to our conference table, and we would have lunch together. The topic of our meetings would ultimately shift to discussions about the Lord.

After the completion of the office building, we continued to meet periodically, at the conference table for "lunch," discussing things about God and Jesus Christ. Turns out, Jerry had been involved in a bible study fellowship for quite some time. Our discussions were candid and honest, seeking to hear each other's thoughts and understandings of the bible. This letter is a result of one of those lunchtime discussions. I hope, as you read this letter, that you will feel as if you are part of this conversation, because you are.

"Jimaky" James Edwin

ONE

THE PREDICAMENT

Dear Jerry,

Since having lunch together and talking about God's justice, these thoughts just won't go away—especially since your voicemail suggesting that I write them down. I've been thinking about it. The Holy Spirit has been adding to the scriptures we had discussed! I think I had better write this down! But, Jerry, before I get too far along, I need to point out something that the apostle Paul said to his young protégé, Timothy. It was in Paul's second letter to his student, and it is thought to be one of his last, if not the very last letter he wrote. Paul encouraged Timothy to be a good steward of God's Word. In other words, to be careful that what he said was true to what God had already said. That's my prayer.

I don't want to screw this up by stretching or manipulating what God has already revealed to us in the scriptures to make them say what I want them to say. So, Father, here is my prayer: Please keep me on track with your truth. And, Jerry, I'm trusting that He will use you to crack the whip if I get out of line. That's a roundabout way of saying that if I do mess up, it will be partly your fault. Ha! I love you, man.

God's justice is a lofty subject, and my legal understanding of justice, much less God's justice, is about as deep as the paper I'm writing on. But though I am not a lawyer or a theologian, I feel like the Holy Spirit moved our discussion along a logical path from scripture to scripture. When Jesus said, in John's gospel, that He is the way to God, that He is the truth of God, and that He is the life of God in the flesh, it seems obvious that we should listen up. However, when I read the Bible, I often come across verses that I tend to skim over, not really stopping to consider what they are saying. For example: Psalm 9:7–8 (NIV) says, "The Lord reigns forever; He has established His throne for judgement. He will judge the world in righteousness; He will govern the peoples with justice."

Obviously, this verse speaks of God's justice. At least the verse says that God has established His throne for judgement. I think that means that God is doing—or plans to do—some judging. But it also says He will judge the world. That would be all of us. And it goes further to say that He will judge the world in righteousness. I believe that means there will be no funny business or trickery. Nobody will be framed for some false accusation. On the flip side, nobody will get away with lying to God by presenting false evidence. The implication is that God's justice will be honest and straightforward. But what's this all about, anyway?

The passage in the gospel of John, chapter 3, where Jesus talks with Nicodemus, is huge. I have always considered John 3:16 to be the whole gospel story in a nutshell. But if you read the entire passage, John 3:1–21, you discover that Jesus was revealing several truths that most people back then—and, really, most people today—don't understand. It was obvious that Nicodemus didn't get it. But, Jerry, I don't think we truly get it either.

In the Bible passages that follow, I will identify which translation is being used. I sometimes prefer different translations, which I will explain later. Most of the time, I like to use an early edition of the NIV (New International Version, 1985). But on occasions, I prefer the old KJV (King James Version) that I received back in 1954 when I accepted Jesus at the age of eight and was baptized. I still have that old bible they gave to me back then. But here goes:

John 3:1–21 (NIV, emphasis mine):

> Now there was a man of the Pharisees named Nicodemus, a member of the Jewish ruling council. He came to Jesus at night and said, "Rabbi, we know you are a teacher who has come from God. For no one could perform the miraculous signs you are doing if God were not with Him." In reply Jesus declared, "I tell you the truth, no one can see the Kingdom of God unless he is born again." "How can a man be born when he is old?" Nicodemus asked. "Surely he cannot enter a second time into his mother's womb to be born!" Jesus answered, "I tell you the truth, no one can enter the Kingdom of God unless he is born of water and the Spirit. Flesh gives birth to flesh, but the Spirit gives birth to spirit. You should not be surprised at my saying, 'you must be born again.' The wind blows wherever it pleases. You hear its sound, but you cannot tell where it comes from or where it is going. So it is with everyone born of the Spirit." "How can this be?" Nicodemus asked. "You are Israel's teacher," said Jesus, "and you do not understand these things? I tell you the truth, we speak of what we know, and we testify to what we have seen, but still you people do not accept our testimony. I have spoken

to you of earthly things and you do not believe; how then will you believe if I speak of heavenly things? No one has ever gone into heaven except the one who came from heaven—the Son of Man. Just as Moses lifted up the snake in the desert, so the Son of Man must be lifted up, that everyone who believes in Him may have eternal life. For God so loved the world that He gave His one and only Son, that whoever believes in Him may have eternal life. For God did not send His Son into the world to condemn the world, but to save the world through Him. *Whoever believes in Him is not condemned, but whoever does not believe stands condemned already because he has not believed in the name of God's one and only Son.* This is the verdict: Light has come into the world, but men loved darkness instead of light because their deeds were evil. Everyone who does evil hates the light, and will not come into the light for fear that his deeds will be exposed. But whoever lives by the truth comes into the light, so that it may be seen plainly that what he has done has been done through God."

Jerry, there's a lot being said by Jesus here. Many of us have probably read it before and may be familiar with it. But thinking about the discussion we had at lunch, look at verse eighteen in italics. Jesus points out the problem right there, and it's a big problem for a lot of people! He is saying that if people don't believe in this Son of God or Son of Man who would be "lifted up," then they stand condemned already! Seriously? At the time, when Jesus said this to Nicodemus, He was saying that virtually everyone walking on the face of the earth was already condemned. This seemed very confusing for Nicodemus, and it may be for us as well!

Nicodemus had already identified Jesus as a teacher who had come from God. In addition, he says this identity had been verified by miraculous signs. *Jesus is not denying this.* Jesus goes further to identify this "one who has come from God" with the bronze serpent Moses held up before the Israelites in the desert for their healing from the bite of the serpent. As the Israelites looked upon the bronze serpent, they lived (Numbers 21:4–9)! But we should not miss the amazing point that Jesus is making here. In this short encounter with Nicodemus, Jesus is spilling the beans about who He is and His purpose for being here. For those who would look to the Son of Man when He would be lifted up, that is, when He would be crucified on the cross, if they believed in Him, they would receive *eternal* life! Wow! This is getting deep but think of how Nicodemus must have felt.

Nicodemus had not yet lived to see Jesus crucified by the Romans. He would later play a role in removing Jesus from the cross and in His burial (John 19:39). And there is the matter of the empty tomb after three days. I'm sure Nicodemus became aware of Jesus's resurrection, and I would assume he was one of the many, over five hundred people, according to the apostle Paul, who saw Jesus before His ascension. But now, before all of this happened, his understanding of Jesus would have been very limited since his picture of Jesus was incomplete. However, Jesus didn't fault Nicodemus for not understanding His identity. *He faulted him for not understanding the basic problem of humankind.* Jesus was saying that everyone was spiritually dead and needed spiritual rebirth to see and enter the Kingdom of God. This kingdom is evidently a realm where God's authority is truly recognized, and He governs the whole show. The kingdom is the king's domain.

Jesus described those citizens as being "born of His Spirit" and moving about freely as the Spirit moves them.

Can this really be true? Is humankind already condemned without having this Son of Man as its savior? And if so, how did this happen? Jesus didn't explain the cause. It appears that He expected Nicodemus to already know the reason why. He pointed out that Nicodemus was a teacher of Israel and that he should understand this situation from his own studies of the Torah.

Jerry, both you and I were chasing after this "rabbit" while we talked during our lunch together. *Understanding this predicament is basic to our understanding of Jesus, God's justice, and His amazing grace.* Hopefully the Holy Spirit will lead us to a place of greater understanding of who Jesus is, what He did, and why He did it. But maybe the most important point is why it had to be Him. *Jesus Christ is the only one who could have done what He did.*

TWO

A LIVING SOUL

Jesus has declared that we must be born again spiritually. When He said this to Nicodemus, it's evident that Jesus expected him to understand why from what he had been taught in the Law, Psalms and Prophets. This is our "Old Testament" today. Back then, it was all that Nicodemus had, and yet, according to Jesus, it was sufficient to give him an understanding of humanity's situation. Let's look and see. And where best to start than at the beginning, in the first book of the Torah—the book of Genesis, and the creation of humanity. There are two passages that deal specifically with the creation of humans, and both are unique, and yet, equally significant.

Genesis 1:26–27 (NIV) says, "Then God said, 'Let us make man in our image, in our likeness, and let them rule over the fish of the sea and the birds of the air, over livestock, over all the creatures that move along the ground.' So God created man in His own image, in the image of God He created him; male and female He created them."

This first passage describes humanity's creation as a kind of climax or crowning achievement. The whole of the creation days or events culminates with this final creature that not only has the "breath of life," as the animals do, but is also created in the image or likeness of its creator. As part of our created being, we actually have a "heart for God" or a "place created for God" in our lives. And this creature is then appointed chief creature, as the ruler and caretaker of all creation.

Jerry, I think being created in the image or likeness of God means that we can relate to Him and communicate with Him better than any other creature. I'm pretty sure cows don't pray.

Genesis 2:7 (KJV) says, "And the Lord God formed man of the *dust of the ground*, and breathed into his nostrils the *breath of life*, and man became a *living soul*." (emphasis mine)

This is the second passage dealing with the creation of humanity, and this one is crucial to the understanding of what Jesus said to Nicodemus. This is one of those places where I prefer to read it in the old King James Version (KJV). I think, if you read this in other versions, you'll see what I mean. This verse, in the KJV, makes it very clear as to who made what "alive"! There are three separate elements, in italics for emphasis, pictured here: First is the body made from the dust of the ground or the physical elements of the creation. The second is the breath of God that breathed into the nostrils of this physical body. And third, when this happened, the text says man became a "living soul."

The Hebrew word for the breath of life here is *Neshamah*. This word is used in this context as God being a breath, but the Hebrew thought implies much more than a movement of air into a body-shaped shell. The result reveals something much more, *a living soul*! It's no stretch to say that this is the Holy Spirit entering into the physical body. *This is the physical encountering the Spiritual. This is God's creation of humanity and our initial Spiritual birth.*

I would like to mention something concerning this biblical narrative, Jerry. It is in regard to God's creation of Adam and from Adam's own flesh, God's creation of Eve. I believe it's clear that all of humanity finds its source in these two initial human beings. And yet, in the sequence of events, Adam was created first, put in the garden of Eden and given the command to not eat of the tree of the knowledge of good and evil. Immediately after giving him the command, we learn of God's creation of Eve from Adams own flesh. Here is my point in this. In His wisdom, when God spoke the command to Adam He spoke to Eve as well, because she was 'in' Adam. And if you will accept it, I believe He was speaking to all of us for the same reason, we were all 'in' Adam. It's from this perspective that I sometimes use the term mankind interchangeably with humankind or humanity. From Genesis 1:27 to Joel 2:28-29 to Acts 2:17-18 it's clear that God's redemption is for all of us, male and female.

It also seems evident, from Genesis 1:30, that all living creatures have God's breath of life. It's what makes them, and us, alive! I believe this is why, in the physical sense, humans have a kind of inherent similarity with animals. We are all living creatures with the ability to move about within the greater created environment, but there is a huge difference between us and all other creatures. When God breathed into this creature, *made in His image,* the result was amazing. Here is where I prefer to read this passage in the KJV because it says, "man became a *living soul*" (emphasis mine). This result is unique to those creatures created in the image of God! We are made *living* souls by the eternal Spirit of God, and the key description of this soul is *living.* I believe this *living soul* is the image of God that He desires for each of us to display in this world! It's His life revealed in and shared with our lives.

Isaiah 60:21b (NIV) says, "They are the shoot I have planted, the work of My hands, for the display of My splendor."

So, Jerry, back then, in the beginning, we *knew* our creator and could communicate with Him directly, as evident by the exchange in Genesis 3:8. Our living souls were meant to communicate and relate to God. Jesus would later describe this *knowledge of God* as *eternal life.* John 17:3 (NIV) says, "Now this is eternal life: that they may know You, the only true God, and Jesus Christ, whom You have sent."

He is eternal God, and we were meant to be His eternal compadres. So, what happened?

THREE

SEPARATED FROM LIFE

It looks like it all started in the garden of Eden. I think we know this story, but it doesn't hurt to walk through it again. And maybe this time, we should stop and consider what really took place. God put man into a garden and gave him some instructions: "And the Lord God took the man and put him in the garden of Eden to dress it and to keep it. And the Lord God commanded the man, saying, 'Of every tree of the garden thou mayest freely eat. But of the tree of the knowledge of good and evil, thou shalt not eat of it, for in the day that thou eatest thereof thou shalt surely die" (Genesis 2:15–17, KJV).

This is another verse that I prefer to read in the KJV because it seems to describe the consequence of disobedience a little more clearly to me than some of the other versions. "For *in the day* that thou eatest thereof thou shalt surely die." This version seems a little more specific about the timing of the consequence for disobedience. The command does not seem overly burdensome. It should have been simple to obey. After all, the whole garden must have been a beautiful and amazing place, safe to explore and enjoy. It was just this one tree. But, not only that, to disobey was unthinkable because the consequence was unimaginable, *death*! What was death? This is the first mention of death in the Bible, *and it's the penalty for disobedience*!

The Bible doesn't give an outright definition of death here, and maybe the author, who most believe was Moses, did not consider this needed explaining. For me, I think the simple definition of death is the "separation from life." And in the context of the biblical narrative, it seems to mean the penalty for disobeying God is separation from God. This makes sense because He is the one who breathed into us the "breath of life," and we became living souls. God is the one who gave us life in the first place. He is, therefore, the source of life. If we believe that life is some kind of commodity, *something separate from God*, and that we can take it and simply walk away from Him, I believe experience proves that we are making a huge mistake.

By giving us this command, God has actually given us the freedom to love Him or not. I have often heard it said that, without this freedom, love for God would be robotic and not genuine. John 14:21a (NIV) says, "Whoever has My commands and obeys them, he is the one who loves Me." We are free to obey or disobey, to love God or not to love God. But there are consequences in either case.

Obviously, we would expect God's continued presence and fellowship if we obey Him and heed His warnings. But if we choose to disobey Him, we are stepping out from under His authority, choosing to go in another direction. We choose to leave Him. Simply put, depending upon which choice is made, the result is either life or death. Genesis 3 gives us the story known as the fall of humanity. It's the story of Eve, and then of Adam, making their choices. And as we know, their choice was to disobey God.

So, Jerry, when I read through this narrative about Eve and Adam doing what God had commanded them not to do, I find myself looking for the "smoking gun." Where is the death that God said would happen *in the day that thou eatest thereof*? We know from reading further in Genesis that Adam and Eve had children. Genesis 5:5 even says that Adam lived 930 years and then died! That's a lot of living after the day that they disobeyed God's command!

But death is there, in the story of Genesis 3. It may not appear, at first, as death to us, if we only understand death as our physical death. But the death they experienced that day was the death of *their souls*. You might think I'm way off base here, Jerry. But consider the description of our creation and our living soul being the product of the Holy Spirit entering our physical body. *Their removal from the garden of Eden as a result of their disobedience is a clear picture of their separation, body and soul, from God's life-giving presence.* Their disobedience broke their personal fellowship with their Creator. And I believe this is clearly the "death" God spoke of in His command. This Spiritual death has resulted in the need for our Spiritual rebirth, as Jesus was saying to Nicodemus.

We don't know how much time passed before the incident with the serpent, but I like to think that there was a period of time before the fall, when they were able to explore things that God had shown them. It's clear from Genesis that, during that period, they had direct fellowship with God. And if there was ever a time when humanity experienced life as God intended for us to experience, it must have been then. Don't you know that those days were filled with amazing adventures!

All of this changed when they disobeyed God's command. When that happened, they suffered the consequences that God had described as death. And it happened on that very day, when they were removed from the garden of Eden. Because of their disobedience, they were separated from God, their source of life. The Holy Spirit that dwelt within them and had given them life was now silent. He was the One with whom they had communicated and through whom they had found their purpose.

Now banished from the garden and God's presence, they no longer had access to the tree of life and no hope of restoring it. As Jesus was saying to Nicodemus, in this state of separation from God, we are condemned to an existence separated from God's Holy Spirit, His fellowship, and the life He wanted us to experience with Him.

Over time, for many, even God's very existence would come into question. Without ongoing fellowship with our eternal life-giver, our physical death eventually occurs, and our bodies of dust return to the earth. Some might think that we simply cease to exist at the end of our physical lives. But the scriptures make it clear, that is not the case. Being created in the image of our eternal God, we are eternal creatures. We will exist with God forever or we will exist without God forever. It should be obvious, Jerry; God wants us to be with Him (Deuteronomy 30:19)! And it should also be clear that if the predicament existed back in the time of Nicodemus, it still exists today. Jesus was saying that unless one is "born of water" or made "clean from sin" and then filled with God's Holy Spirit or "born again Spiritually," he or she could not truly experience God's fellowship and walk with Him in His realm. The flesh cannot produce God's Spirit. The flesh can only give birth to flesh.

At first glance, it appears that this predicament cannot be undone unless God goes back on His word and winks at our disobedience, ignoring our guilt by sweeping our sins under the rug. If God did that, how would you feel, Jerry? What would you think about God's character? It's obvious our sins are not something that can be ignored. They have broken our fellowship with our Creator, and it must be fixed. *It's a matter of eternal life or eternal death.* Because of God's righteous sovereignty and holy nature this penalty of death would have to be satisfied and not ignored.

Jerry, this is where you raised a good, but tough, question to answer satisfactorily. You asked, "Did God make a mistake in giving us free will?" I wish I could give an answer that would satisfy the believer, the nonbeliever, and everyone else whose perspective is somewhere in between. The answer is to be found throughout the Bible, even in the passage in John where Jesus spoke to Nicodemus. But God has led me to the book of Habakkuk, where the prophet seemed to echo your question: Habakkuk 1:13 (NIV) says, "Your eyes are too pure to look on evil; you cannot tolerate wrong. Why then do you tolerate the treacherous?" And Habakkuk 2:4b (NIV) goes on to say, "but the righteous will live by his faith."

This takes some explaining, and we need to look at some other scriptures:

Galatians 3:14 (NIV) says, "He redeemed us in order that the blessing given to Abraham might come to the Gentiles through Christ Jesus, so that by faith we might receive the promise of the Spirit." The blessing given to Abraham was righteousness as a result of his believing God. Romans 4:3 (NIV) says, "What does the scripture say? 'Abraham believed God and it was credited to him as righteousness.'" (This references Genesis 15:6.)

Jerry, the apostle Paul was saying that we are given righteousness by faith in Jesus Christ. That God's grace! And this righteousness is necessary so that we may receive God's Spirit and be Spiritually born again. This all happens, as God said to Habakkuk, *by faith*. He is telling us to *trust Him* throughout the entire Bible!

So, what does this have to do with your question? I believe God is telling us the answer is, no! He makes no mistakes, *but we do*! He is telling us to trust Him. It's obvious from scripture that God is grieved by the sin and brokenness brought about by humankind. (Genesis 6:6) Yes, there are casualties because of our sins, but He is in the process of redeeming His creation.

Should God have made us as robots who had no choice but to love Him? Absolutely not! In that state, we would *not* be created in His image. Genuine love requires the freedom to not love. Genuine love is faithful love despite the circumstances. And, Jerry, here is something that I think we often overlook. The difficulty in answering your question reveals, I believe, our inabilities to fully comprehend God. We are made recipients of His amazing grace and love as a result of our exercising the freedom to *not* love Him. Despite our sinfulness, God has chosen to love us anyway, and He has established a way, even a covenant, that offers forgiveness of our sins and restoration into His fellowship. This happens not by ignoring our sins, but by removing them from those who will believe and receive this gift of grace *by faith.* As we will see, God's love is truly on display in His response to our rebellion. We would have never known the extent of God's love, had we not sinned.

Isaiah 55:9 (NIV) says, "As the heavens are higher than the earth, so are My ways higher than your ways and My thoughts than your thoughts."

FOUR

DEAD MEN WALKING

Jerry, have you ever considered this? The penalty of immediate death, or the death "in the day that you eatest of it," isn't really mentioned specifically in Genesis 3. We see it carried out in the expulsion from the garden and the resulting separation from God's presence and the tree of life. This penalty of death takes place, but it isn't mentioned outright. However, we do read about the resulting curses and judgements it brings.

There is the curse of the serpent and the curse of the ground, and there are judgements or resulting conditions that are described regarding the serpent, the woman, and the man. But for our discussion about God's justice, have you noticed that these curses and judgements are regarding the *days to come*, including future generations through childbirth? Looking back at God's warning that "in the day that you eat of it, you will surely die", things obviously did not come to a screeching halt and explode into nonexistence! These conditions describe what we would call our normal experiences in life today, such as painful childbirth and hard work. God has given us time to live even without our direct fellowship with Him! But for what reason? *It appears that God is not finished with us!*

There are a couple of things that come to mind when I think about this. First, God allows our physical lives to continue, and second, He does set a limit. I see both as examples of God's loving mercy and grace. Consider this: even in our fallen state, God wants us to know and experience His creation. This universe is an expression of God's glory. I know that sounds very religious, but if you will find a place where you can turn off the noise and really look beyond the pollution, you will see its beauty and grandeur. Hopefully you'll recognize it as God's handiwork.

And with regard to the limited time that we are given here, it does appear that God has made some adjustments in the past. At first, the life spans seem unbelievable, such as Adam living 930 years. But later, in Genesis 6:3 (NIV), we read, "Then the Lord said, 'My Spirit will not contend with man forever, for he is mortal; his days will be a hundred and twenty years.'" And later still, in Psalm 90:10 (NIV), we read, "The length of our days is seventy years—or eighty, if we have strength; yet their span is but trouble and sorrow, for they quickly pass, and we fly away."

God first reduced humanity's life spans to 120 years, saying His Spirit would not contend with them forever. But since God sees the evil of our hearts in Genesis 6:5–6, it looks like He reduced our life spans even further, to seventy or maybe eighty years. I don't mean to imply that these numbers are absolute requirements or limits, but *they appear to be another picture of God's grace and mercy.* The psalmist says humanity's experience is full of trouble and sorrow, and perhaps God wanted to shorten this pain.

It might be helpful to read a couple of passages regarding this separation from God and the resulting pain it brings. Jerry, the event described in the garden of Eden may seem like a minor violation, *but the result has proven to be catastrophic.*

First,

Genesis 6:5–6 (NIV) says,

"The Lord saw how great man's wickedness on the earth had become, and that every inclination of the thoughts of his heart was only evil all the time. The Lord was grieved that He had made man on the earth, and His heart was filled with pain."

Isaiah 59:1–4, 7–8 (NIV) says:

Surely the arm of the Lord is not too short to save, nor His ear to dull to hear. But your iniquities have separated you from your God; your sins have hidden His face from you, so that He will not hear. For your hands are stained with blood, your fingers with guilt. Your lips have spoken lies, and your tongue mutters wicked things. No one calls for justice; no one pleads his case with integrity. They rely on empty arguments and speak lies; they conceive trouble and give birth to evil. … Their feet rush into sin; they are swift to shed innocent blood. Their thoughts are evil thoughts; ruin and destruction mark their ways. The way of peace they do not know; there is no justice in their paths. They have turned them into crooked roads; no one who walks in them will know peace.

The reason we should obey God is not so much of a mystery after reading those passages. And sadly, the truth of them is verified by the current events of today. As the old saying goes, "hindsight is 20/20," and we can only shout a warning to Eve and Adam from their distant future. But by God's grace, we are given time to live in our physical bodies before we eventually die our physical deaths. But, Jerry, without interaction with God's

Holy Spirit, before our physical deaths, we are literally *dead men walking,* spiritually speaking. It's what Jesus meant when He told Nicodemus we were condemned already.

This could have been the end of God's great plan. But thankfully, it's just the beginning. From this point of humanity's separation from God, the Bible begins what has been called the greatest story ever told. It also could be called, God's amazing scheme to redeem.

FIVE

THE VERDICT IS IN

When Jesus spoke with Nicodemus about mankind's need for Spiritual rebirth, He spoke with authority. He had witnessed the whole story unfold from the very beginning when He said the verdict was in. Humanity's guilt was confirmed by their actions. Perhaps, if they had only been discussing Adam and Eve, maybe Nicodemus could have seen that the problem began with their removal from God's presence. Using a light-versus-dark metaphor, with God's Holy Spirit being the light that gave humanity life and purpose, Nicodemus still failed to see that humankind's light needed to be restored and that their separation from God had spread to all of us. Their darkness had become *our* darkness.

And now Jesus was saying that God's light had stepped back into the world as this Son of Man, *revealing God's righteous sovereignty, as well as His loving grace.* This revelation of God acted as a light shining in the dark. And it was exposing the sinfulness of humanity. He told Nicodemus that this Son of Man would provide the way back into a new relationship with God. But He also said that many had grown so accustomed to their self-centered ways that they would reject this light, preferring to hide or even deny their evil deeds rather than live in truth and righteousness.

When Jesus said this Son of Man would provide the way for

humankind to have access into the presence of God, He gave an image of how it would be done, comparing it to the Old Testament account of Moses lifting up the bronze serpent (Numbers 21:8–9). Jerry, I think this is where we began to examine God's justice a little closer and where we begin to examine Jesus a little more intently.

After a verdict is rendered in a trial, a judgement is then issued by the judge. A guilty verdict will result in the judgement or sentence as defined by the law or prescribed by the judge. In the Genesis account, Adam and Eve both confessed their guilt (Genesis 3:12–13). So, we know in their case that the verdict was guilty. And according to Jesus, that guilt has continued through the generations, infecting all of humanity (John 3:19). So, if the verdict is guilty, what about the judgement? Look at this verse in Hebrews 9:27 (NIV): "Just as man is destined to die once and *after that to face judgement*" (emphasis is mine).

Jerry, this verse is something to ponder. Think about what this is saying. It's one of those Bible verses that speaks of an undeniable truth. Even if one does not believe in God, here is something on which we can all agree. As repulsive as this may sound, we're all going to die. This is obviously speaking of our physical deaths. Jesus has made it clear that we are already dead, *Spiritually speaking*, and in need of a Spiritual rebirth. But in the same breath, this verse says that, after our physical deaths, *there is a judgement*! This really got my attention when I first saw this. But there's more: as the Bible reaches its final few pages, we are given a vivid picture of this judgement: Revelation 20:14–15 (NIV) explains, "Then death and Hades were thrown into the lake of fire. The lake of fire is the second death. If anyone's name was not found written in the Book of Life, he was thrown into the lake of fire."

Yikes! The apostle John has written down what he saw in his vision, trying to describe something extremely difficult to comprehend. I don't think this is something he could make up. I think he's trying to say that death, this separation from God, is finally going to be removed from God's creation, completely! Death and anything and everything connected with it, including the deceiver, will be gone. There have been many things speculated about hell. I have even heard of some who accuse God of being unjust and unloving for sending people there. I would want those to understand that God doesn't send anyone to hell. *They send themselves.*

Honestly, it should be obvious that life was created by the life-giver, and to live life *as He intended it* is not possible apart from Him. Yet, many folks have been deceived into believing they can. They believe they can live life centered around themselves as the supreme authority. They have chosen to step away from the genuine life-creator. But even so, God still loves them. In fact, the Bible is all about God's efforts to save His creation from the predicament humankind has created. He loved us even after we had turned our backs on Him. Romans 5:8 (NIV) says, "But God demonstrates His own love for us in this: While we were still sinners, Christ died for us."

Jerry, the mention of judgement after our physical death is important. I think it suggests the possibility of a favorable outcome, as well as an unfavorable outcome! This declaration that there will be a judgement after our physical death, actually offers hope to our predicament. It hints that there may be a way to get back into the garden and have access to that tree of life! Wouldn't that be a favorable outcome? But what does this judgement mean? And, most importantly, how would you go about achieving a favorable outcome? Jesus gave the answer to Nicodemus in John 3:16 (NIV): "For God so loved the world that He gave His one and only Son, that whoever believes in Him shall not perish but have eternal life."

Eternal life! That's the favorable outcome we're looking for. That means returning to the garden and the tree of life. Jesus called it Paradise to the thief on the cross (Luke 23:43). It means a restored relationship with our Creator, God! But here is where we began to shift gears. Why does believing in Jesus provide us with a favorable judgement? What did Jesus do? What does it mean to *believe* in Jesus? We both agree that it must mean to believe the things He said. We believe that He is the truth, and we rely on what He did for us. And there's the question: What *did* Jesus do for us? I know He died on the cross for my sins, but how did His death gain a favorable judgement for me when the verdict against me is already "guilty"?

SIX

JUDGEMENT'S COMING

Judgement is a judicial decision having to do with the administration of justice. Ha! That's a mouthful, and it sounds like double-talk! But the decision in context here is the execution of the sentence described by the demands of the law. And we are talking about God's judgement, as well as His justice, as it pertains to this "fall of humanity" described in the Bible.

I have a friend who is a federal judge. I asked him if judgement was the same as reaching a verdict. He explained that the verdict was the decision that determined whether a person was guilty or not guilty. Depending upon the verdict, the judgement or judicial decision would then affirm or disaffirm (deny) whether a debt or obligation to the law had been created. If the debt was affirmed, the judge would follow up with a sentence that declares what punishment or payment would be inflicted, levied, or imposed on the guilty person to satisfy the incurred debt. My point is this: there seems to be a period of time between the rendering of a verdict, where guilt is determined, and the final judgement, where the sentence is carried out. Jerry, it may sound like I am splitting hairs, but I think this period of time between the verdict and the judgement is where our *hope* lies.

Justice has been illustrated for centuries by the statue of Lady Justice. She is often blindfolded to represent impartiality or justice without prejudice—no bribes here! She holds a sword to represent the decisiveness of a just decision, slicing between what is just and unjust. True justice unveils truth. But perhaps the most telling image is that she is holding a set of scales that are perfectly balanced.

To me, the balanced scales best represent the "penalty" and the "payment". Consider this illustration: A governing authority recognizes the potential for a dangerous accident to occur when people drive through an intersection without first stopping to look for oncoming traffic. To protect its citizens, it creates a law that says people must stop at intersections where a stop sign is installed, and they will then determine a penalty that must be paid if this law is broken. If someone breaks this law by driving through the intersection without stopping, he or she must pay the price of the penalty. Until that penalty is paid, the scales of justice are out of balance and the sovereignty and authority of the governing body is being challenged or pushed aside. Once that penalty is paid, the scales return to the balanced position and the governing authority retains its sovereignty. A "payment" was made that equaled or fully satisfied the "penalty" determined by the governing body. In biblical justice, it's fair to say that God is the governing body!

From His initial command to Adam on down to our present day, God's sovereignty has continually been pushed aside by our own choices. We shouldn't forget, from the very beginning, the penalty for disobeying God's commands or laws is *Spiritual death*! And for His sovereignty to be reinstated, a payment must be made that will forever satisfy that penalty. Jerry, this is where we began to see that what Jesus did was something only He could have done.

To understand this more clearly, it would help to look at Old Testament justice:

> If anyone takes the life of a human being, he must be put to death. Anyone who takes the life of someone's animal must make restitution—life for life. If anyone injures his neighbor, whatever he has done must be done to him: fracture for fracture, eye for eye, tooth for tooth. As he has injured the other, so he is to be injured. Whoever kills an animal must make restitution, but whoever kills a man must be put to death. You are to have the same law for the alien and the native born. I am the Lord your God. (Leviticus 24:17–22, NIV)

It's often said that this Old Testament law and others similar to it are limited to the Old Testament. Some believe that, today, God is all about love, forgiveness, and turning the other cheek. I do think that's true, but God has not changed His mind about those laws. And yet, He *is* all about love, forgiveness, and turning the other cheek. *It's why He sent Jesus.*

Jesus would speak of this Old-Testament justice in a revolutionary new way:

> You have heard that it was said, eye for eye, and tooth for tooth. *But I tell you*, do not resist an evil person. If someone strikes you on the right cheek, turn to him the other also. And if someone wants to sue you and take your tunic, let him have your cloak as well. If someone forces you to go one mile, go with him two miles. Give to the one who asks you, and do not turn away from the one who wants to borrow from you. You have heard that it was said, love your neighbor and hate your enemy. But I tell you: love your enemies and pray for those who persecute you, that you may be

sons of your Father in heaven. He causes His sun to rise on the evil and the good, and sends rain on the righteous and the unrighteous. If you love those who love you, what reward will you get? Are not even the tax collectors doing that? And if you greet only your brothers, what are you doing more than others? Do not even pagans do that? *Be perfect, therefore, as your heavenly Father is perfect.* (Matthew 5:38–48, NIV; emphasis is mine)

This passage is about midway in Jesus's Sermon on the Mount. In it, the bible says the crowd was amazed at His teaching because He taught as one who had authority, not as their usual teachers of the law. And here, in this passage, Jesus says something astonishing. Without striking down these Old-Testament laws as being unjust, He simply tells us we should not seek the retribution they demand! Instead, we are to turn the other cheek and love our enemies. This is hardcore forgiveness. And then, Jesus ends by raising the bar way out of reach for any of us. Perfect? Who on earth could truly live like that? It turns out, Jesus could and *did*!

By showing us God's extreme standard of mercy and forgiveness, Jesus is revealing not only God's amazing love and grace; by contrast, He shows us the depth of our own fallen nature. Here is where, I think, we often miss the boat concerning Jesus. This revelation of God's holy standard is intended *to reveal our absolute need for Jesus*. This isn't a new set of laws that we are supposed to keep on our own; these are standards we are unable to fulfill without God's Holy Spirit dwelling in us. They're impossible without being born again, Spiritually. It's what Jesus was saying to Nicodemus!

Things seemed hopeless for me when I first read Jesus's words—maybe because my scales of justice were really out of whack. But as time went by, I began to see Jesus in a brighter light. This is why God stepped into His creation. It's why He took on flesh as the Son of Man. Something had to be done about this penalty of death that our sins had brought into our lives. Without God's Holy Spirit, we couldn't even begin to keep the standard of perfection Jesus proclaimed. And if that penalty is not paid, this verdict of guilt and the resulting separation from God will continue with us all the way through our physical death to our final judgement and eternal separation from God!

If only our penalty could be paid before we stand before the judge!

SEVEN

VENGEANCE IS MINE

Jerry, when I heard that Jesus said I am not supposed to seek the retribution that the Old-Testament laws demand, I struggled to understand why. If I have suffered a wrong that has hurt me deeply, forgiveness can be extremely difficult. We all know that. But if you imagine yourself in the crowd, watching Jesus and hearing Him say those impossible words, *and then you look ahead to His death, burial, and resurrection*, it puts our situation in a completely new perspective.

Of course, I am supposed to forgive others because I have been forgiven through the sacrifice of Jesus Christ on that cross! If God forgives me for my sins by sacrificing His own Son, why on earth should I not forgive someone who has sinned against me? *I must forgive others because God has forgiven me!* Mark 11:25 (NIV) says, "And when you stand praying, if you hold anything against anyone, forgive him, so that your Father in heaven may forgive you your sins."

But, Jerry, there's something else. There's another reason why we should forgive and not seek the retribution demanded by those Old-Testament laws. Look at Genesis 3:15 (NIV): "And I will put enmity between you and the woman, and between your offspring and hers; He will crush your head, and you will strike His heel." Deuteronomy 32:43 (NIV) also says, "Rejoice, O nations, with

His people, for he will avenge the blood of His servants; He will take vengeance on His enemies and make atonement for His land and people." Isaiah 1:24 (NIV) says, "Therefore the Lord, the Lord Almighty, the Mighty One of Israel, declares: 'Ah! I will vent my wrath on My foes and avenge Myself on My enemies.'"

And in the New Testament, Romans 12:19 (NIV) says, "Do not take revenge, my dear friends, but leave room for God's wrath, for it is written: 'It is mine to avenge; I will repay,' says the Lord."

It's clear that we are to forgive those who sin against us because *it's God's prerogative to seek the retribution against evil, not us*! If we refuse to forgive and attempt to get revenge, we only kick the can farther down the road. God wants that flame to be snuffed out in each of us. Why? He wants us to know life, not death. How? By putting everything in His hands. God's got this!

Look at Genesis 3:15 again. God is speaking to Satan, the deceiver, represented by the serpent in the Genesis story. Here, God discloses His intention for the deceiver, declaring that He will send this One (Jesus), this "enmity" between good and evil. This One will certainly be "bruised in His heel" by this deceiver; but this One will give the deceiver a "head crushing." That's a death blow! *That's vengeance against the evil deceiver.* And God is making this declaration! The deceiver is ultimately responsible for the evils of this world. God's vengeance would be accomplished by this One whom He would send, *not by you or me*. This One would be the only full manifestation of God given in the flesh, hence, the "only begotten" Son. He has been given many titles, but here we see Him most importantly as the Son of Man. *He really was God in the flesh!*

Note that God's vengeance against evil is directed toward the deceiver. *Humankind is not the primary target of God's vengeance.* On the contrary, God's vengeance not only achieved final victory over the deceiver (the "head crushing"), but God's vengeance will also gain our freedom from the death penalty demanded by His own command. How? *God would choose to take our death penalty Himself!* This was the "heel crushing" inflicted by the deceiver. The guilty verdict, which came with our disobedience, and the final penalty of death, God paid Himself, in human form, as the Son of Man, Jesus Christ. What appeared to be a defeat, God turned into victory over the devil.

We were told that He was going to do this from the words of Abraham: Genesis 22:8 (KJV) says, "And Abraham said, my son, God will provide Himself a lamb for a burnt offering: so they went both of them together." The prophet Isaiah also says, "We all, like sheep, have gone astray, each of us has turned to our own way; and the Lord has laid on Him the iniquity of us all. He was oppressed and afflicted, yet He did not open His mouth; He was led like a lamb to the slaughter, and as a sheep before its shearers is silent, so He did not open His mouth. By oppression and judgement, He was taken away. Yet who of His generation protested? For He was cut off from the land of the living; for the transgression of My people, He was punished" (Isaiah 53:6–8, NIV).

From the words of John the Baptist, "The next day John saw Jesus coming toward him and said, 'Look, the Lamb of God, who takes away the sin of the world'" (John 1:29, NIV). Since the beginning of the Bible (Genesis 3:15), it has been God's plan to avenge the work of the devil. In 1 John 3:8b (NIV), it says, "The reason the Son of God appeared was to destroy the devil's work."

Jerry, Christ's death included not only His physical death but also the death of His soul! His death would include the separation from His Father. We know that happened from His final words on the cross. Matthew 27:46, 50 says, "About the ninth hour Jesus cried out in a loud voice, 'Eloi, Eloi lama sabachthani' [which means, "My God, My God, why have you forsaken Me?"] … And when Jesus had cried out again in a loud voice, He gave up

His Spirit." John 19:30 (NIV) says, "When He had received the drink, Jesus said, 'It is finished.' With that, He bowed His head and gave up His Spirit."

His death paid the penalty required by God's command given to Adam, and ultimately to all of us, because we were all "in" Adam at the time it was spoken. The payment of Jesus Christ's life, including His living soul, fully satisfied the death penalty for all of us! *This is the life for life demanded by the old law!*

We had no way of redeeming ourselves because the verdict of guilt was already on us. *Our souls were already dead*—that is, we were already separated from God's holy presence because of our sins. Jesus made that clear when He was talking with Nicodemus. Separated from God's Holy Spirit at the garden of Eden, we all lacked the life necessary to pay the full penalty demanded by God's decree. The verdict of guilty was in; we were already "dead men walking," awaiting our final judgement. Our only hope would be someone *Spiritually alive*, who was willing to offer up His own living soul as payment for our dead souls. It would take a "live man walking" to balance the scales of justice!

EIGHT

A LIVE MAN WALKING

Jerry, if you go back to that passage in Isaiah 59, where we saw the outcome of humanity trying to live life separated from God, and read a little further, you see that God would, indeed, step in to save His creation:

Isaiah 59:14–16 (NIV) says, "So justice is driven back and righteousness stands at a distance; truth has stumbled in the streets, honesty cannot enter. Truth is nowhere to be found and whoever shuns evil becomes a prey. *The Lord looked and was displeased that there was no justice.* He saw that there was no one, He was appalled that there was no one to intervene; *so His own arm worked salvation for Him, and His own righteousness sustained Him*" (emphasis is mine).

The commands of God are broken, His sovereignty is ignored, and justice is far from us. Since the day that Eve and Adam disobeyed God's command not to eat from the tree of the knowledge of good and evil, humankind has continued in disobedience. Throughout the generations, the flesh has continued to reproduce flesh, but not the Spirit. The penalty of death that occurred that day in the garden was the *death of our souls*, and *our separation from (eternal) life is in effect.* The scales of justice are out of balance and a payment needs to be made that will bring them back into a balanced position. But that requires a payment of equal value or weight to satisfy the penalty of death. Only then will the scales be balanced and justice fully served. *Until that happens, the sovereignty of God is pushed aside.*

But who could pay this penalty of death? As Jesus said to Nicodemus, every person on earth is already condemned and are "dead men and women walking," spiritually speaking! And as the passage in Isaiah said, there was no one to intervene. The apostle Paul, in the New Testament, echoed Isaiah's message. Romans 3:23 (NIV) says, "For all have sinned and fall short of the glory of God." Further in this book, Romans 6:23 (NIV) says, "The wages of sin is death."

The problem is this, no one on earth had the kind of life necessary to pay for what had been lost, namely the life of our soul, our relationship with God's Holy Spirit. He is the life of our souls (Genesis 2:7), and our souls have been cut off from that life by our own doing (Isaiah 59:2). God's justice requires an equal for an equal, "an eye for an eye" or "a life for a life." The penalty, the sentence of death demanded by the command of God, resulting in the death of the soul, *would require the payment of a living soul* before justice could be satisfied and the scales would be balanced again.

Matthew 16:26 (NIV)_ says, "What good will it be for a man if he gains the whole world, yet forfeits his soul? Or *what can a man give in exchange for his soul?* (emphasis mine) Jesus is pointing to our predicament when He asks this question. And under our fallen condition, what *could* we give in exchange for our lifeless souls? We possessed nothing of equal value!

This brought our discussion to one of the tenets of our Christian faith, the virgin birth. The fact is that the corrupted seed of Adam could never produce a Spiritual human. Jesus clearly said that flesh only gives birth to flesh. But this lineage of corruption was broken by the virgin birth of Jesus Christ! The gospels of

Matthew and Luke both explain that the pregnancy of the Virgin Mary was a miracle brought about by the Holy Spirit. The gospel of John describes Jesus as the Word of God becoming flesh. It is obvious that Jesus, from conception, was a "live man walking." That is, from conception, His soul was in perfect fellowship with the Holy Spirit. And yet, this Son of Man would be birthed into physical life just as we are and would experience life just as we do, beginning as a child and growing into adulthood.

When Jesus was baptized by John the Baptist, John said he saw the Holy Spirit descend upon Jesus in the form of a dove—that is, peacefully. And, Jerry, the fact that it says the Holy Spirit remained on Him signifies that Jesus had not accumulated any sin from birth to baptism! There was nothing to separate Jesus from the Holy Spirit of God!

At that time, He was the only one who walked the earth as a "live man walking," who had a living soul that enjoyed unbroken fellowship with God, the Father! There had been many prophets throughout the Old Testament who had been anointed by God's Holy Spirit, and God had used them in mighty ways. Even John the Baptist was filled with the Holy Spirit from birth (Luke 1:15). But no one, other than Jesus, was born from the seed of God's Holy Spirit in a virgin womb. Jesus described Himself as the Son of Man, so He was fully human, and yet He was called the Son of God by the Father Himself (Matthew 3:17, 17:5).

And here, at the commencement of His ministry, this picture of the baptism of Jesus points to a couple of things. First is our need for His baptism, that is, our cleansing from sin. *Our sins must be removed before it is possible for God's Holy Spirit to indwell us.* His death on the cross accomplished that. His death was our penalty for our sins that He paid in full for us, and, *by faith,* we believe that our sins are completely removed (i.e., we are made clean) by the sacrifice of Jesus on the cross. And second, by that same faith, we believe in the resurrection of Jesus from the dead and receive the same Holy Spirit that brought Jesus out of the grave, restoring His life.

Our souls are restored and made alive by His Holy Spirit. Ephesians 1:13–14 (NIV) says, "And you also were included in Christ when you heard the word of truth, the gospel of your salvation. Having believed, *you were marked in Him with a seal, the promised Holy Spirit*, who is a deposit guaranteeing our inheritance until the redemption of those who are God's possession—to the praise of His glory" (emphasis mine).

As Jesus said to Nicodemus in John 3:5 (NIV), "Jesus answered, 'I tell you the truth, no one can enter the Kingdom of God unless he is born of water and the Spirit." The Old Law, an eye for an eye, a tooth for a tooth, a life for a life, is still in effect today. *The God of the Old Testament has not changed!* So, in the passage from Isaiah 59, we read that God, after seeing that there was no one else, stepped forth as a Son of Man or God in the flesh, to save His creation. God would send this servant, one on whom His Holy Spirit would rest, because He had no sin. He would therefore be a "live man walking," and it would cost this "live man walking" His life, *including His living soul*. This sacrificial offering, this blood sacrifice, satisfied that old law and, at the same time, established a new covenant between God and humanity.

Isaiah 42:1, 6–9 (NIV) says:

> Here is My Servant, whom I uphold, My Chosen One in whom I delight; I will put My Spirit on Him and *He will bring justice to the nations.* ... I, the Lord, have called you in righteousness; I will take hold of your hand. I will keep you and make you to be a covenant for the people and a

light for the Gentiles, to open eyes that are blind, to free captives from prison and to release from the dungeon those who sit in darkness. I am the Lord; that is My Name! I will not give My Glory to another or My Praise to idols. See, the former things have taken place, and New Things I declare; before they spring into being I announce them to you.

Did you notice what it said about justice in that first verse above, in italics? I emphasized this because Jesus *balanced the scales for us* by paying our death penalties! That has been a stunning revelation for me, that God would do a new thing. He's announcing a new covenant; *God would give us another chance at eternal life.* But we would have to believe it to receive it. Just as in the garden, we have a choice to make: "Turn to Me and be saved all you ends of the earth; for I am God and there is no other" (Isaiah 45:22, NIV).

REPENTANCE

Jerry, you may have noticed that I have a special regard for the book of Isaiah. And I do for a couple of reasons. The first is because of all the references concerning the Messiah and the new covenant found in this ancient text. But when I learned that there were several copies of Isaiah, one almost entirely complete that was found among the Dead Sea Scrolls, it really got my attention. This nearly complete copy of Isaiah has been dated to around 200 BC. That's the earliest known copy we have today, and it's very close to being the same as our modern text with only slight variations.

There is another point to be made here. This copy is proof that Isaiah wrote these prophecies centuries *before the time of Jesus.* And yet they describe Him and His death and resurrection *exactly as recorded by the eyewitness accounts of His disciples.*

The scroll of Isaiah begins with the Lord's lament that His children, the Jewish nation of Israel, have turned away from Him, and there are soon-coming judgements announced. And as we saw earlier, Isaiah reveals God's "suffering servant" who will take away the sins of His people. God will introduce a new covenant between Himself and humankind. And He offers this redemption to all people, Jews and Gentiles alike!

Isaiah 49:6 (NIV) says, "It is too small a thing for You to be

39

My Servant to restore the tribes of Jacob and bring back those of Israel I have kept. I will also make You a light for the Gentiles, *that You may bring My salvation to the ends of the earth*" (emphasis mine). Isaiah presents a vivid picture of a Messiah in whom we can *all* take refuge. This is the New Testament gospel revealed in this Old Testament book. But then, in the last chapter of Isaiah, questions are asked: Isaiah 66:8 (NIV) says, "Who has ever heard of such a thing? Who has ever seen such things? Can a country be born in a day, or a nation be brought forth in a moment? Yet no sooner is Zion in labor than she gives birth to her children."

This text is an ancient prediction concerning the future return of Zion. It speaks of the rebirth of the long-lost nation of Israel, *before they were lost!* This prophecy was written before the Babylonian exile and way before the Romans destroyed the second temple and scattered the Jews in AD 70. Isaiah lived approximately eighty-one years (740–681 BC) and was a significant prophet during the reign of Hezekiah, King of Judah (715–686 BC). Why would God preserve this copy of Isaiah along with most of the other Old Testament books in these Dead Sea Scrolls, and then allow them to resurface after two thousand years, during the exact same time period that the nation of Israel was actually being restored (1947–1948)? This is *obviously* not a coincidence! God seems to be waving a big flag here. The world should listen up! I think He wants us to pay attention to these things.

So, with that said, take a look at the following verses. Isaiah 59:20–21 (NIV) says, "'The Redeemer will come to Zion, *to those in Jacob who repent of their sins,*'" declares the Lord. 'As for Me, this is *My Covenant with them,*' says the Lord. 'My Spirit, who is on you, and My words that I have put in your mouth will not depart from your mouth or from the mouths of your children or from the mouths of their descendants from this time on *and forever,*' says the Lord" (emphasis is mine). This verse is saying that God's

Spirit, who is on this Redeemer (a.k.a. servant), as well as God's Word or teachings that He has put in Him, will never leave Him or His children or their descendants, *forever*! That's the covenant God is making with those "in Jacob" *who repent of their sins*! God is making a contract with those who change their minds about their sinful behaviors. And this contract will be administered by and through this Redeemer. God's covenant with them is this: His Spirit and the words He has spoken through this Redeemer will never depart from them. Jerry, *that's Spiritual rebirth*. I believe this is one of those passages Jesus thought Nicodemus should have understood.

And again, to be clear, God had already said He would, through this Redeemer or servant, offer this salvation to *all* people. I mention this because the text says the covenant will be with those "in Jacob," which might be understood as excluding everybody else. But this is an indication of God reaching out to the Jews first. The Redeemer did indeed come to Zion first, to those "in Jacob." This was God's order in the scheme of things. But after reading this verse and hearing what Isaiah said about *those with whom God would make this new covenant*, it would be helpful for us to take a good look at the word *repent*. This new covenant will be with those who repent of their sins!

The Greek word that is translated into English for *repentance* is *metanoia*, which simply means "to change your mind." My dictionary defines *repent* as, "to feel such remorse or regret for past conduct as to change one's mind regarding it" (*The American Heritage Dictionary of the English Language* 1969).

This definition implies a change of mind about my conduct, but it only seems to say that I now recognize my guilt. Nothing here really speaks of how to get rid of my guilt or how to change my conduct! Yet, this definition is important to understand! If I fail to *truly* change my mind about what is sinful in my life and fail to agree with God and believe what He says is sin, I simply won't repent. I won't see the need, because I love the darkness more than the light. This is what Jesus was saying to Nicodemus.

In my early understanding of repentance, it meant more about changing my ways than changing my mind. I thought I had to change my ways before God would accept me. So, whenever I would hear a pastor preach on repentance I would immediately jump onto a strict path of legalism, trying to keep all the rules, something I was never successful in doing. There have been many times when I had to confess my frustrations and say to God, "I can't live like this!" And I believe that's exactly what God wanted me to realize. I need a Savior!

Repentance, in Isaiah's passage, does imply a change of mind regarding my life. But in this biblical context, repentance is a realization that my sins have turned me away or separated me from God. It's a recognition of sin as sin! And these folks, according to Isaiah, are the ones the Redeemer is approaching. But, Jerry, changing my mind about sinful behavior is not enough. Biblical repentance is never about mind over matter or thinking my way into righteousness. Biblical repentance is recognizing my sins and my need for the Redeemer and His redemption. Recognizing my sins, without the love and forgiveness of the Redeemer and His transforming power, can lead to anger and frustration or regret and remorse over my guilt. It can lead to denial, self-loathing, or worse. The Redeemer is the key figure here in biblical repentance. John 14:6 (NIV) says, "Jesus answered, 'I am the way and the truth and the life. No one comes to the Father except through Me.'"

And there's something else about biblical repentance that we should understand. It appears that all of us, to one degree or another, needs help to recognize and change our minds about our sins. We should consider the grip they may hold on our lives. The fact that we may love our sins does not change the fact that they will ultimately destroy us. And God does not want that to happen to anyone. 2 Peter 3:9 (NIV) says, "The Lord is not slow in keeping His promise, as some understand slowness. Instead, He is patient with you, not wanting anyone to perish, but everyone to come to repentance."

Here are a couple of verses that reveal an integral part of *biblical* repentance: John 6:44 (NIV) says, "No one can come to Me unless the Father who sent Me draws him, and I will raise him up at the last day." And as His time was getting closer to the cross, Jesus would later say, "But I, when I am lifted up from the earth, will draw all men to Myself" (John 12:32, NIV). Both verses are describing *biblical* repentance—that is, they imply a turning to Jesus Christ, who is the Redeemer! And both mention a "drawing". I believe this is describing one of the major roles of God's Holy Spirit on the earth.

On the night of the Last Supper, before Jesus was arrested, He spoke to His disciples about things that would soon take place. He described the coming of the Holy Spirit as the comforter, counselor, advocate, or helper. But He also spoke of the Holy Spirit bringing conviction of guilt: "When He comes, He will convict the world of guilt in regard to sin and righteousness and judgement: in regard to sin, because men do not believe in Me; in regard to righteousness, because I am going to the Father, where you can see Me no longer; and in regard to judgement, because the prince of this world now stands condemned" (John 16:8–11, NIV).

Humanity is guilty of sin because of our disobedience to God's laws, and the Holy Spirit will remind us of this. The world will see the righteousness of Christ when they see the empty tomb, His resurrection from the dead, and His return to the Father. His righteousness is a witness, in contrast, to our guilt. He sits in the presence of God while the world does not. The Holy Spirit reveals that the death penalty has been paid for all who are in Christ, but the prince of this world, and all who remain with him, stand condemned just as Jesus said to Nicodemus.

Jerry, it will take the Holy Spirit to reveal these things. It will take the Holy Spirit to bring us to repentance. It will take the Holy Spirit to help us change our minds about our sin and the Redeemer. Philippians 2:13 (NIV) says, "For it is God who works in you to will and to act according to His good purpose."

But unfortunately, many will still not believe, resisting the truth, preferring the darkness over the light. This biblical repentance not only changes our minds about our sin but also changes our minds about Jesus. The Holy Spirit, while opening our eyes to reveal the harmful nature of sin, will also point us to the forgiveness and redemption available in Jesus Christ. Jesus offers His righteousness to all who repent or change their minds about their sins and turn to Him for the power to live this new life. He has secured this salvation *for all who will turn to Him and believe His message.*

John 1:12–13 (NIV) says, "Yet to all who did receive Him, to those who believed in His name, He gave the right to become children of God—children born not of natural descent, nor of human decision or a husband's will, but born of God."

TEN

THE TIME HAS COME

At the entrance to the New Testament, this call for repentance is heard loud and clear. This is where we meet John the Baptist, who is considered the last Old Testament prophet in the bible. John's father, Zechariah, sang a prophetic song over his newly born son:

Luke 1:76–79 says, "And you my child shall be called a prophet of the Most High; for you will go on before the Lord to prepare the way for Him, to give His people the knowledge of salvation through the forgiveness of their sins, because of the tender mercy of our God, by which the rising sun will come to us from heaven to shine on those living in darkness and in the shadow of death, to guide our feet into the path of peace."

John came preaching a strong message about changing our minds concerning sin! Luke 3:2–6 (NIV) says:

> During the high priesthood of Annas and Caiaphas, the word of God came to John, son of Zechariah, in the desert. He went into all the country around the Jordan, preaching a baptism *of repentance for the forgiveness of sins.* As is written in the book of the words of Isaiah the prophet: "A voice of one calling in the desert, prepare the way for the Lord, make straight paths for Him.

> Every valley shall be filled in, every mountain and hill made low. The crooked roads shall become straight, the rough ways smooth. And all mankind will see God's salvation." (emphasis mine)

Matthew 3:5–12 (NIV) says:

> People went out to him from Jerusalem and all Judea and the whole region of the Jordan. Confessing their sins, they were baptized by him in the Jordan River. But when he saw many of the Pharisees and Sadducees coming to where he was baptizing, he said to them: You brood of vipers! Who warned you to flee from the coming wrath? *Produce fruit in keeping with repentance.* And do not think you can say to yourselves, "We have Abraham as our father." I tell you that out of these stones God can raise up children for Abraham. The ax is already at the root of the trees and every tree that does not produce good fruit will be cut down and thrown into the fire. I baptize you with water for repentance. But after me will come One who is more powerful than I, whose sandals I am not fit to carry. He will baptize you with the Holy Spirit and with fire. His winnowing fork is in His hand and He will clear His threshing floor, gathering His wheat into the barn and burning up the chaff with unquenchable fire. (emphasis mine)

I can't help but think that John was remembering that passage in Isaiah 59:20–21 when he preached "repentance for the forgiveness of sins" to the people. He was literally telling them to "change their minds" about the sin in their lives because this Redeemer, the one Isaiah had spoken about *more than five hundred years earlier* was now entering the earth. Indeed, John was announcing that He was already here: "The next day John saw Jesus coming toward him and said, 'Look, the Lamb of God, who takes away the sin of the world'" (John 1:29, NIV).

The time had come for God's people, those "in Jacob," to repent of their sins! John was baptizing those who had truly changed their minds about their lives. If there was ever a time when God was drawing people, it was surely there. It seems evident that God was speaking through John the Baptist and the Holy Spirit was moving the repentant folks deeply. And they expressed their remorse by being baptized by John, desiring the cleansing or purification symbolized by washing in the waters of the Jordan River.

But, Jerry, we all know that we can resist this message! It's not unusual for many to resist the message to repent. This is the battleground where lives are won or lost. For many, this whole notion of God and sin and the message of the Bible sounds so bizarre, they refuse it because they simply don't believe it. Or, for some reason, they don't *want* to believe it. This is why Jesus said it was hard for the rich to enter the kingdom of God. Those who are insulated from the curses of the world by wealth in its various forms are often satisfied with their comforts, pleasures, protections, or powers and don't see the need to be saved from anything.

This may be why John spoke such condemning words to the Pharisees and Sadducees when he recognized their hypocritical hearts and unchanging arrogance. They evidently believed that simply because they were descendants of Abraham, their acceptance by God was a sure thing, giving them a false sense of security and even superiority. Their hypocrisy obviously angered him. John's message made it clear that God's judgement was near, "The axe is already at the root of the trees." This warning was to repent and recognize their sinful ways. His message was to change their minds about their sinful pride, but evidently their arrogance, along with their positions of authority, held a tight grip on their lives.

This need for repentance isn't something found only in the New Testament. David knew the importance of repentance before God: "The sacrifices of God are a broken spirit; a broken and contrite heart, O God, You will not despise" (Psalm 51:17, NIV). But John's message of repentance *did include something new!* John would present a *new* covenant to the people of God! He would put a name on this new covenant and present *Jesus* as the final Lamb of God offered for those who would repent of their sins. Years ago, the Old Testament prophets had prophesied that God would do something different, something new in their future. Isaiah spoke of God declaring "new things" (Isaiah 42:9). And Jeremiah revealed that God would "make a new covenant" (Jeremiah 31:31). And Ezekiel, a prophet living in exile in Babylon, prophesied to Israel that God would give them a "new heart" and "put a new spirit" in them. (Ezekiel 36:26)

Jerry, these Old Testament passages from Isaiah, Jeremiah and Ezekiel were in the Jewish scrolls *centuries before the time of John the Baptist.* God's desire had always been for His children to simply turn and trust in Him, but history had shown that they would not. Isaiah 30:15 (NIV) says, "This is what the sovereign Lord, the Holy One of Israel says: 'In repentance and rest is your salvation, in quietness and trust is your strength, but you would have none of it.'"

John's message of repentance, considering what the prophets had already said, was not new. But the time had now come, and the servant or Redeemer was about to fulfill those ancient prophecies! God was about to bring His justice to the nations and put a new covenant in place. It would solve humankind's sin problem and allow His children back into His presence *without compromising His righteous requirements of the Law.*

Indeed, the way of God's soon-coming judgement was also God's soon-coming grace! For the soon-coming judgement, of which John spoke, would fall upon his cousin*, Jesus, the "Lamb of God that takes away the sin of the world." This perfect Lamb, without defect, without sin, this "live man walking," would give His living soul as payment for the death penalty our sins had incurred. Jesus would pay our debt for us.

Note: *John's mother, Elizabeth, was a relative of Mary, the mother of Jesus (see Luke 1:36.) The exact relationship between John and Jesus isn't known, and the term *cousin* is only meant to imply a family connection.

ELEVEN

THE DEBT IS PAID

Jerry, we began our discussion about God's justice with the passage in John's gospel where Jesus spoke with Nicodemus. And the more I think about it, the more I believe this passage is the most definitive narrative explaining the desperate purpose for the entire bible. It is the elephant in the room. Let me rephrase that—it's the elephant in the universe!

I recently watched a video portrayal of this encounter between Jesus and Nicodemus and this excellent rendition had taken some liberties to give the scene an image of reality while remaining true to the biblical text. And in it, Jesus spoke of conquering sin, not the Roman Empire. This was the revelation that the disciples struggled to understand even after His resurrection: "Then they gathered around Him and asked Him, 'Lord, are you at this time going to restore the kingdom to Israel?" (Acts 1:6, NIV).

We know that sin is the name of that elephant. And it's what Jesus expected Nicodemus to understand! And I think it's what He wants all of us today to understand as well. Sin has pervaded the creation so much for so long that it has blinded us all. It's difficult to imagine an existence without it. But that's where God wants to take us, back to that life. It's the true life that God created us to experience, life that can only exist with Him. And to be with our Creator requires that which separates us to be removed. The sin debt, *which is death*, must be paid. And it will be paid by each of us unless someone else pays it for us. Either way, the penalty of death, prescribed by God in His command to Adam—and subsequently to each of us—must be satisfied. The debt will be paid.

The crucifixion of Jesus is where God's justice was accomplished. This is where the debt was paid and the scales of justice were balanced for you and me! The picture of Jesus, nailed to the cross is such a powerful image. But there was much more going on besides Christ's physical execution. The real death of Jesus, His true separation from life, was the absence of His heavenly Father! As the Son of Man, the soul of Jesus experienced something He had never experienced before, separation from His Father. Isaiah 53:11 (NIV) says, "After the suffering of His soul, He will see the light of life and be satisfied; by His knowledge My righteous Servant will justify many, and He will bear their iniquities." This verse says it all.

Jerry, this was our penalty! This is the debt we have incurred, and Jesus took it upon Himself. This "separation from the Father" is something you and I, who have turned to this Redeemer and believed and received His sacrificial death as payment for our own debt, will *never* have to suffer, not even for an instant, when we die our physical deaths. Jesus has paid that penalty for us. Hebrews 2:9 (NIV) says, "But we see Jesus, who was made a little lower than the angels, now crowned with glory and honor because He suffered death, so that *by the grace of God He might taste death for everyone.*" (emphasis is mine)

Since we know, and scripture declares, that we are all going to die our physical deaths (Hebrews 9:27), this death that Jesus tasted for all of us is the second death referred to in the Book of Revelation (Revelation 20:6, 14). This is the judgement where the sentence is carried out.

When He lifted the cup of wine during the last supper and said, "This is My blood of the covenant which is poured out for many for the forgiveness of sins," (Matthew 26:28), He would have brought to the disciple's remembrance a passage of scripture from the Book of Leviticus. In this passage Moses established the Day of Atonement where the repentant Israelites received forgiveness of sin by a blood sacrifice. Leviticus 16:34 (NIV) says, "This is to be a lasting ordinance for you. Atonement is to be made once a year for all the sins of the Israelites. And it was done as the Lord commanded Moses." Leviticus 17:11 (NIV) further says, "For the life of a creature is in the blood and I have given it to you to make atonement for yourselves on the altar; it is the blood that makes atonement for one's life."

This blood sacrifice of Jesus, offered up for our sins, covered the sentence of death, even the death of our souls. Jesus was willing to go through this on our behalf. This was God's will because of His love for each of us. And it is another picture of Jesus fulfilling the Old Testament law.

Matthew 5:17 (NIV) says, "Do not think that I have come to abolish the Law or the Prophets; I have not come to abolish them but to fulfill them."

Jerry, God has accepted this sacrifice as payment for our sins. How do I know that? By Christ's resurrection. Jesus had no sin that would have resulted in His own death so there was nothing to keep Him in the grave. His death was a voluntary act of accepting *our* sins upon Himself. And when He did that, He suffered the consequences of sin which is death, even Spiritual death, for us. Three days in eternity, from our perspective, was evidently sufficient to pay our debts in full, and by His own authority He rose from the dead!

John 10:17–18 (NIV) says, "The reason My Father loves Me is that I lay down My Life—only to take it up again. No one takes

it from Me, but I lay it down of My own accord. I have authority*
to lay it down and authority to take it up again. This command
I received from My Father."

(*Note: the KJV says *power* instead of *authority*.)

The Book of Hebrews, chapter 8, speaks of Jesus as our high
priest and in Hebrews 9:12 (NIV) it says, "He did not enter by
means of the blood of goats and calves; but He entered the Most
Holy Place once for all by His own blood, having obtained eternal
redemption." Jesus came to us as our high priest *and* our sacrifice.
And the redemption that has been obtained for us, is *eternal*! This
is forever! This is amazing!

As you said Jerry, when we believe and accept this reality for
our own lives, God's Holy Spirit "shows up"! When we are 'born
again' Spiritually we are no longer "dead men walking," and
our new, eternal lives begin. In 1 Peter 1:23 (KJV) the apostle
Peter said, "Being born again, not of corruptible seed, but of
incorruptible, by the word of God, which liveth and abideth
forever." Peter was saying that we begin a new life in Christ as
infants learning how to navigate in this kingdom of God. And
even though I have lived in this realm for some time now I am
still holding on to his hand, learning how to walk and hopefully
bear the fruit of His presence in my life.

Galatians 5:22 (NIV) says, "But the fruit of the Spirit is love,
joy, peace, patience, kindness, goodness, faithfulness, gentleness
and self-control. Against such things there is no law."

One of the great things about bearing these "fruits" is that
they are a natural product of this new nature. We don't need to
try to fake it, but we do need to keep our roots tapped into Him.
We must stay connected to Jesus.

John 15:4 (NIV) says, "Remain in Me and I will remain in

you. No branch can bear fruit by itself; it must remain in the vine. Neither can you bear fruit unless you remain in Me."

Jerry, we know this transition is often met with resistance from our old way of living. The old nature doesn't want to lay down without a fight. But when the struggles begin, remember the victory over death, that "separation from God," has been removed by Jesus Christ on the cross. We now, in Christ, have His Holy Spirit with us. *We are not alone. It's by His victory and power that we now live.*

John 16:33 (NIV) says, "I have told you these things, so that in Me you may have peace. In this world you will have trouble. But take heart! I have overcome the world." Do I completely understand or comprehend all that God has done and is doing in my life? Absolutely not. But I trust Him with my life. And I know He is trustworthy! This journey is not finished, but my faith and hope are in the One who knows the way.

Philippians 1:6 (NIV) says, "Being confident of this, that He who began a good work in you will carry it on to completion until the day of Christ Jesus."

Jerry, if you and I were to condense our discussion down to a few simple words, I know we would agree:

Jesus Christ *is* God's justice!

God loves us my friend! Let's do lunch.

"Jimaky" James Edwin

POSTSCRIPT

For anyone else who might find this letter and read it, I hope you will look at these verses from the bible in the light of what Jesus has done for us:

- Psalm 34:22 (NIV): "The Lord redeems His servants; no one will be condemned who takes refuge in Him."
- Isaiah 28:16–17a (NIV): "See, I lay a stone in Zion, a tested stone, a precious cornerstone for a sure foundation; the one who trusts will never be dismayed. I will make *justice* the measuring line and *righteousness* the plumb line." (emphasis is mine)
- Romans 5:16–17 (NIV): "Again, the gift of God is not like the result of the one man's sin: *The judgement followed one sin and brought condemnation*, but *the gift followed many trespasses and brought justification*. For if, by the trespass of the one man, death reigned through that one man, how much more will *those who receive* God's abundant provision of grace and of the gift of righteousness reign in *life* through the one man, Jesus Christ!" (emphasis is mine)
- 1 Corinthians 1:30 (NIV) "It is because of Him that you are in Christ Jesus, who has become for us wisdom from God—that is, our righteousness, holiness and redemption."

You might notice in the last verse above that Jesus has become our righteousness, our holiness, and our redemption—the standard that we could never achieve on our own because we were "dead men walking," Jesus is for us. And He will give us His righteousness and all the rest if we just ask Him. I hope you will.

Romans 10:12–13 (NIV) says, "For there is no difference between Jew and Gentile—the same Lord is Lord of all and richly blesses all who call on Him, for everyone who calls on the name of the Lord will be saved."

REFERENCE LIST

William Morris, Editor. 1969. The American Heritage Dictionary of the English language. New York: American Heritage Publishing Co., Inc., page 1103, 'repent'. Def 2

A NOTE FROM JERRY

We all have a past. And sometimes the choices we have made appear to be unmovable roadblocks to any hopeful future. But the Bible says, "We are saved by grace through faith." Saved … from what? Saved *for* what? This little book shows us how to remove those roadblocks and reveals the path to not only a renovated future, but a renovated soul. When invited, the Holy Spirit shows up. I know. This letter was written to me. And to you.

Jerry

A WORD ABOUT MY PEN NAME

My parents both grew up on farms in Western Oklahoma during the time of the Great Depression, the Dust Bowl, and World War II. Life was hard, but during the early days of their marriage, things became even more difficult as they experienced three separate, full-term pregnancies, each ending with the birth of baby girls. Due to illness, each of my sisters died within a few days of their births. At the doctor's advice, my parents were told not to attempt to have any more children. The trauma of losing three babies was just too much.

In February of 1941, they adopted my brother. In December of that same year, Pearl Harbor was bombed and World War II began. Mom and Dad, along with my big brother, moved to Oregon, where Dad worked in the shipyards helping build battleships for the war. After the war ended, they moved back to Oklahoma, where I was born on my big brother's fifth birthday. I always thought it was neat having the same birthday as my big brother.

My dad's father died during those war years, and his mom followed soon after that. Not knowing my dad's parents, my only grandpa was my mom's dad. I still have three memories of him from my younger days. They left "forever" marks in my heart. My grandpa was a wheat farmer. In a year of drought, I remember being with him in a field of dry dirt as he knelt down to tenderly touch a small sprout of wheat. Even at my young age of three or four years, I could sense his love for the land and his hope for rain. In the second memory I have of him, I see him standing in his living room while Mom, Dad, and Mom's sister and her two brothers, along with the rest of us kids, watched in tears as he described the last few minutes of Grandma's life on this earth. She had died, and we had all gathered for her funeral.

My last memory of Grandpa is of when we were all going on a trip somewhere. I had crawled up into the back seat of our old car, not knowing that Grandpa was coming in behind me. As he sat down next to me, he reached out and patted me on the knee and exclaimed, "Oh, Jimaky," with a loving smile. That was it! I would forever be "Jimaky," because when he said it, I knew that my grandpa loved me. That may sound a little odd, but as I look back on the struggles my parents had, I have come to realize that my grandpa struggled and felt the same pain that his youngest daughter had when she lost those three baby girls. I chose this pen name to honor my grandpa, and, in a roundabout way, to honor my mom and dad. James is my first name; Edwin (Grandpa's name) is my middle name. So, "Jimaky" James Edwin is my pen name.

Printed in the United States
by Baker & Taylor Publisher Services